Candle Making Journal

LOGBOOK INFORMATION

Start Date	
End Date	

OWNER INFORMATION

Name	
Address	
Phone Number	
Email Address	

QUICK RECAP

NAME / DESCRIPTION	OVERALL RATING	LOG PAGE

NAME / DESCRIPTION	OVERALL RATING	LOG PAGE

DATE CREATED _____

CANDLE NAME	

INGREDIENTS	AMOUNT	METHOD SUMMARY
		....
		....
		....
		....
		....
		....
		....
		....
		....
		....
		....
		....
		....
		....
		....
		....
		....
		....

OILS & SCENTS	MOLD & FINISH

OVERALL RATING									
1	2	3	4	5	6	7	8	9	10

IMAGE(S) / SKETCHES

NOTES / SUGGESTIONS FOR IMPROVEMENT

BURN LENGTH RATING

1	2	3	4	5	6	7	8	9	10

DATE CREATED _____

CANDLE NAME	

INGREDIENTS	AMOUNT	METHOD SUMMARY

OILS & SCENTS	MOLD & FINISH

OVERALL RATING									
1	2	3	4	5	6	7	8	9	10

IMAGE(S) / SKETCHES

NOTES / SUGGESTIONS FOR IMPROVEMENT

BURN LENGTH RATING

1	2	3	4	5	6	7	8	9	10

DATE CREATED _____

CANDLE NAME	

INGREDIENTS	AMOUNT	METHOD SUMMARY

OILS & SCENTS	MOLD & FINISH

OVERALL RATING									
1	2	3	4	5	6	7	8	9	10

IMAGE(S) / SKETCHES

NOTES / SUGGESTIONS FOR IMPROVEMENT

BURN LENGTH RATING

1	2	3	4	5	6	7	8	9	10

DATE CREATED _____

CANDLE NAME	

INGREDIENTS	AMOUNT	METHOD SUMMARY

OILS & SCENTS

MOLD & FINISH

OVERALL RATING

1	2	3	4	5	6	7	8	9	10

IMAGE(S) / SKETCHES

NOTES / SUGGESTIONS FOR IMPROVEMENT

BURN LENGTH RATING

1	2	3	4	5	6	7	8	9	10

DATE CREATED _____

CANDLE NAME	

INGREDIENTS	AMOUNT

METHOD SUMMARY

OILS & SCENTS

MOLD & FINISH

OVERALL RATING

1	2	3	4	5	6	7	8	9	10

CANDLE CREATION LOG

IMAGE(S) / SKETCHES

NOTES / SUGGESTIONS FOR IMPROVEMENT

BURN LENGTH RATING

1	2	3	4	5	6	7	8	9	10

DATE CREATED _____

CANDLE NAME	

INGREDIENTS	AMOUNT	METHOD SUMMARY

OILS & SCENTS	MOLD & FINISH

OVERALL RATING									
1	2	3	4	5	6	7	8	9	10

IMAGE(S) / SKETCHES

NOTES / SUGGESTIONS FOR IMPROVEMENT

BURN LENGTH RATING									
1	2	3	4	5	6	7	8	9	10

DATE CREATED _____

CANDLE NAME	

INGREDIENTS	AMOUNT	METHOD SUMMARY

OILS & SCENTS	MOLD & FINISH

OVERALL RATING									
1	2	3	4	5	6	7	8	9	10

IMAGE(S) / SKETCHES

NOTES / SUGGESTIONS FOR IMPROVEMENT

BURN LENGTH RATING

1	2	3	4	5	6	7	8	9	10

DATE CREATED _____

CANDLE NAME	

INGREDIENTS	AMOUNT	METHOD SUMMARY

OILS & SCENTS	MOLD & FINISH

OVERALL RATING

1	2	3	4	5	6	7	8	9	10

IMAGE(S) / SKETCHES

NOTES / SUGGESTIONS FOR IMPROVEMENT

BURN LENGTH RATING

1	2	3	4	5	6	7	8	9	10

CANDLE CREATION LOG

DATE CREATED _____

CANDLE NAME	

INGREDIENTS	AMOUNT	METHOD SUMMARY

OILS & SCENTS	MOLD & FINISH

OVERALL RATING

1	2	3	4	5	6	7	8	9	10

IMAGE(S) / SKETCHES

NOTES / SUGGESTIONS FOR IMPROVEMENT

BURN LENGTH RATING

1	2	3	4	5	6	7	8	9	10

CANDLE CREATION LOG

DATE CREATED _____

CANDLE NAME	

INGREDIENTS	AMOUNT	METHOD SUMMARY

OILS & SCENTS	MOLD & FINISH

OVERALL RATING									
1	2	3	4	5	6	7	8	9	10

IMAGE(S) / SKETCHES

NOTES / SUGGESTIONS FOR IMPROVEMENT

BURN LENGTH RATING

1	2	3	4	5	6	7	8	9	10

DATE CREATED _____

CANDLE NAME	

INGREDIENTS	AMOUNT	METHOD SUMMARY

OILS & SCENTS	MOLD & FINISH

OVERALL RATING
1	2	3	4	5	6	7	8	9	10

IMAGE(S) / SKETCHES

NOTES / SUGGESTIONS FOR IMPROVEMENT

BURN LENGTH RATING

1	2	3	4	5	6	7	8	9	10

DATE CREATED _____

CANDLE NAME	

INGREDIENTS	AMOUNT	METHOD SUMMARY

OILS & SCENTS	MOLD & FINISH

OVERALL RATING									
1	2	3	4	5	6	7	8	9	10

IMAGE(S) / SKETCHES

NOTES / SUGGESTIONS FOR IMPROVEMENT

BURN LENGTH RATING

1	2	3	4	5	6	7	8	9	10

CANDLE CREATION LOG

DATE CREATED _____

CANDLE NAME	

INGREDIENTS	AMOUNT	METHOD SUMMARY

OILS & SCENTS	MOLD & FINISH

OVERALL RATING

1	2	3	4	5	6	7	8	9	10

IMAGE(S) / SKETCHES

NOTES / SUGGESTIONS FOR IMPROVEMENT

BURN LENGTH RATING

1	2	3	4	5	6	7	8	9	10

DATE CREATED _____

CANDLE NAME	

INGREDIENTS	AMOUNT	METHOD SUMMARY

OILS & SCENTS	MOLD & FINISH

OVERALL RATING									
1	2	3	4	5	6	7	8	9	10

IMAGE(S) / SKETCHES

NOTES / SUGGESTIONS FOR IMPROVEMENT

BURN LENGTH RATING

1	2	3	4	5	6	7	8	9	10

DATE CREATED _____

CANDLE NAME	

INGREDIENTS	AMOUNT	METHOD SUMMARY

OILS & SCENTS	MOLD & FINISH

OVERALL RATING									
1	2	3	4	5	6	7	8	9	10

IMAGE(S) / SKETCHES

NOTES / SUGGESTIONS FOR IMPROVEMENT

BURN LENGTH RATING

1	2	3	4	5	6	7	8	9	10

CANDLE CREATION LOG

DATE CREATED _____

CANDLE NAME	

INGREDIENTS	AMOUNT	METHOD SUMMARY

OILS & SCENTS	MOLD & FINISH

OVERALL RATING									
1	2	3	4	5	6	7	8	9	10

IMAGE(S) / SKETCHES

NOTES / SUGGESTIONS FOR IMPROVEMENT

BURN LENGTH RATING

1	2	3	4	5	6	7	8	9	10

CANDLE CREATION LOG

DATE CREATED _____

CANDLE NAME	

INGREDIENTS	AMOUNT	METHOD SUMMARY

OILS & SCENTS	MOLD & FINISH

OVERALL RATING

1	2	3	4	5	6	7	8	9	10

IMAGE(S) / SKETCHES

NOTES / SUGGESTIONS FOR IMPROVEMENT

BURN LENGTH RATING

1	2	3	4	5	6	7	8	9	10

DATE CREATED _____

CANDLE NAME	

INGREDIENTS	AMOUNT

METHOD SUMMARY

OILS & SCENTS

MOLD & FINISH

OVERALL RATING									
1	2	3	4	5	6	7	8	9	10

IMAGE(S) / SKETCHES

NOTES / SUGGESTIONS FOR IMPROVEMENT

BURN LENGTH RATING

1	2	3	4	5	6	7	8	9	10

DATE CREATED _____

CANDLE NAME	

INGREDIENTS	AMOUNT	METHOD SUMMARY

OILS & SCENTS	MOLD & FINISH

OVERALL RATING

1	2	3	4	5	6	7	8	9	10

IMAGE(S) / SKETCHES

NOTES / SUGGESTIONS FOR IMPROVEMENT

BURN LENGTH RATING

1	2	3	4	5	6	7	8	9	10

CANDLE CREATION LOG

DATE CREATED _____

CANDLE NAME	

INGREDIENTS	AMOUNT	METHOD SUMMARY

OILS & SCENTS	MOLD & FINISH

OVERALL RATING

1	2	3	4	5	6	7	8	9	10

IMAGE(S) / SKETCHES

NOTES / SUGGESTIONS FOR IMPROVEMENT

BURN LENGTH RATING

1	2	3	4	5	6	7	8	9	10

CANDLE CREATION LOG

DATE CREATED _____

CANDLE NAME	

INGREDIENTS	AMOUNT	METHOD SUMMARY

OILS & SCENTS	MOLD & FINISH

OVERALL RATING									
1	2	3	4	5	6	7	8	9	10

IMAGE(S) / SKETCHES

NOTES / SUGGESTIONS FOR IMPROVEMENT

BURN LENGTH RATING

1	2	3	4	5	6	7	8	9	10

DATE CREATED _____

CANDLE NAME	

INGREDIENTS	AMOUNT	METHOD SUMMARY

OILS & SCENTS	MOLD & FINISH

OVERALL RATING

1	2	3	4	5	6	7	8	9	10

IMAGE(S) / SKETCHES

NOTES / SUGGESTIONS FOR IMPROVEMENT

BURN LENGTH RATING

1	2	3	4	5	6	7	8	9	10

DATE CREATED _____

CANDLE NAME	

INGREDIENTS	AMOUNT	METHOD SUMMARY

OILS & SCENTS	MOLD & FINISH

OVERALL RATING									
1	2	3	4	5	6	7	8	9	10

IMAGE(S) / SKETCHES

NOTES / SUGGESTIONS FOR IMPROVEMENT

BURN LENGTH RATING

1	2	3	4	5	6	7	8	9	10

DATE CREATED _____

CANDLE NAME	

INGREDIENTS	AMOUNT	METHOD SUMMARY

OILS & SCENTS	MOLD & FINISH

OVERALL RATING									
1	2	3	4	5	6	7	8	9	10

IMAGE(S) / SKETCHES

NOTES / SUGGESTIONS FOR IMPROVEMENT

BURN LENGTH RATING

1	2	3	4	5	6	7	8	9	10

CANDLE CREATION LOG

DATE CREATED _____

CANDLE NAME	

INGREDIENTS	AMOUNT

METHOD SUMMARY

OILS & SCENTS

MOLD & FINISH

OVERALL RATING									
1	2	3	4	5	6	7	8	9	10

IMAGE(S) / SKETCHES

NOTES / SUGGESTIONS FOR IMPROVEMENT

BURN LENGTH RATING

1	2	3	4	5	6	7	8	9	10

DATE CREATED _____

CANDLE NAME	

INGREDIENTS	AMOUNT	METHOD SUMMARY

OILS & SCENTS	MOLD & FINISH

OVERALL RATING									
1	2	3	4	5	6	7	8	9	10

IMAGE(S) / SKETCHES

NOTES / SUGGESTIONS FOR IMPROVEMENT

BURN LENGTH RATING

1	2	3	4	5	6	7	8	9	10

DATE CREATED _____

CANDLE NAME	

INGREDIENTS	AMOUNT	METHOD SUMMARY

OILS & SCENTS	MOLD & FINISH

OVERALL RATING									
1	2	3	4	5	6	7	8	9	10

IMAGE(S) / SKETCHES

NOTES / SUGGESTIONS FOR IMPROVEMENT

BURN LENGTH RATING

1	2	3	4	5	6	7	8	9	10

DATE CREATED _____

CANDLE NAME	

INGREDIENTS	AMOUNT	METHOD SUMMARY

OILS & SCENTS	MOLD & FINISH

OVERALL RATING									
1	2	3	4	5	6	7	8	9	10

IMAGE(S) / SKETCHES

NOTES / SUGGESTIONS FOR IMPROVEMENT

BURN LENGTH RATING

1	2	3	4	5	6	7	8	9	10

DATE CREATED _____

CANDLE NAME	

INGREDIENTS	AMOUNT	METHOD SUMMARY

OILS & SCENTS	MOLD & FINISH

OVERALL RATING									
1	2	3	4	5	6	7	8	9	10

IMAGE(S) / SKETCHES

NOTES / SUGGESTIONS FOR IMPROVEMENT

BURN LENGTH RATING

1	2	3	4	5	6	7	8	9	10

CANDLE CREATION LOG

DATE CREATED _____

CANDLE NAME	

INGREDIENTS	AMOUNT	METHOD SUMMARY

OILS & SCENTS	MOLD & FINISH

OVERALL RATING									
1	2	3	4	5	6	7	8	9	10

IMAGE(S) / SKETCHES

NOTES / SUGGESTIONS FOR IMPROVEMENT

BURN LENGTH RATING

1	2	3	4	5	6	7	8	9	10

DATE CREATED _____

CANDLE NAME	

INGREDIENTS	AMOUNT	METHOD SUMMARY

OILS & SCENTS	MOLD & FINISH

OVERALL RATING									
1	2	3	4	5	6	7	8	9	10

IMAGE(S) / SKETCHES

NOTES / SUGGESTIONS FOR IMPROVEMENT

BURN LENGTH RATING

1	2	3	4	5	6	7	8	9	10

CANDLE CREATION LOG

DATE CREATED _____

CANDLE NAME	

INGREDIENTS	AMOUNT	METHOD SUMMARY

OILS & SCENTS	MOLD & FINISH

OVERALL RATING

1	2	3	4	5	6	7	8	9	10

IMAGE(S) / SKETCHES

NOTES / SUGGESTIONS FOR IMPROVEMENT

BURN LENGTH RATING

1	2	3	4	5	6	7	8	9	10

DATE CREATED _____

CANDLE NAME	

INGREDIENTS	AMOUNT	METHOD SUMMARY

OILS & SCENTS	MOLD & FINISH

OVERALL RATING									
1	2	3	4	5	6	7	8	9	10

IMAGE(S) / SKETCHES

NOTES / SUGGESTIONS FOR IMPROVEMENT

BURN LENGTH RATING

1	2	3	4	5	6	7	8	9	10

DATE CREATED _____

CANDLE NAME	

INGREDIENTS	AMOUNT	METHOD SUMMARY

OILS & SCENTS	MOLD & FINISH

OVERALL RATING									
1	2	3	4	5	6	7	8	9	10

IMAGE(S) / SKETCHES

NOTES / SUGGESTIONS FOR IMPROVEMENT

BURN LENGTH RATING

1	2	3	4	5	6	7	8	9	10

CANDLE CREATION LOG

DATE CREATED _____

CANDLE NAME	

INGREDIENTS	AMOUNT	METHOD SUMMARY

OILS & SCENTS	MOLD & FINISH

OVERALL RATING									
1	2	3	4	5	6	7	8	9	10

IMAGE(S) / SKETCHES

NOTES / SUGGESTIONS FOR IMPROVEMENT

BURN LENGTH RATING

1	2	3	4	5	6	7	8	9	10

DATE CREATED _____

CANDLE NAME	

INGREDIENTS	AMOUNT	METHOD SUMMARY

OILS & SCENTS	MOLD & FINISH

OVERALL RATING									
1	2	3	4	5	6	7	8	9	10

IMAGE(S) / SKETCHES

NOTES / SUGGESTIONS FOR IMPROVEMENT

BURN LENGTH RATING

1	2	3	4	5	6	7	8	9	10

DATE CREATED _____

CANDLE NAME	

INGREDIENTS	AMOUNT	METHOD SUMMARY

OILS & SCENTS

MOLD & FINISH

OVERALL RATING

1	2	3	4	5	6	7	8	9	10

IMAGE(S) / SKETCHES

NOTES / SUGGESTIONS FOR IMPROVEMENT

BURN LENGTH RATING

1	2	3	4	5	6	7	8	9	10

CANDLE CREATION LOG

DATE CREATED _____

CANDLE NAME	

INGREDIENTS	AMOUNT	METHOD SUMMARY

OILS & SCENTS	MOLD & FINISH

OVERALL RATING

1	2	3	4	5	6	7	8	9	10

IMAGE(S) / SKETCHES

NOTES / SUGGESTIONS FOR IMPROVEMENT

BURN LENGTH RATING

1	2	3	4	5	6	7	8	9	10

DATE CREATED _____

CANDLE NAME	

INGREDIENTS	AMOUNT	METHOD SUMMARY

OILS & SCENTS	MOLD & FINISH

OVERALL RATING									
1	2	3	4	5	6	7	8	9	10

IMAGE(S) / SKETCHES

NOTES / SUGGESTIONS FOR IMPROVEMENT

BURN LENGTH RATING

1	2	3	4	5	6	7	8	9	10

DATE CREATED _____

CANDLE NAME	

INGREDIENTS	AMOUNT	METHOD SUMMARY
		....
		....
		....
		....
		....
		....
		....
		....
		....
		....
		....
		....
		....
		....
		....
		....
		....
		....
		....
		....

OILS & SCENTS	MOLD & FINISH

OVERALL RATING									
1	2	3	4	5	6	7	8	9	10

IMAGE(S) / SKETCHES

NOTES / SUGGESTIONS FOR IMPROVEMENT

BURN LENGTH RATING

1	2	3	4	5	6	7	8	9	10

CANDLE CREATION LOG

DATE CREATED _____

CANDLE NAME	

INGREDIENTS	AMOUNT	METHOD SUMMARY

OILS & SCENTS	MOLD & FINISH

OVERALL RATING									
1	2	3	4	5	6	7	8	9	10

IMAGE(S) / SKETCHES

NOTES / SUGGESTIONS FOR IMPROVEMENT

BURN LENGTH RATING

1	2	3	4	5	6	7	8	9	10

DATE CREATED _____

CANDLE NAME	

INGREDIENTS	AMOUNT	METHOD SUMMARY

OILS & SCENTS	MOLD & FINISH

OVERALL RATING									
1	2	3	4	5	6	7	8	9	10

IMAGE(S) / SKETCHES

NOTES / SUGGESTIONS FOR IMPROVEMENT

BURN LENGTH RATING

1	2	3	4	5	6	7	8	9	10

DATE CREATED _____

CANDLE NAME	

INGREDIENTS	AMOUNT	METHOD SUMMARY

OILS & SCENTS	MOLD & FINISH

OVERALL RATING									
1	2	3	4	5	6	7	8	9	10

IMAGE(S) / SKETCHES

NOTES / SUGGESTIONS FOR IMPROVEMENT

BURN LENGTH RATING

1	2	3	4	5	6	7	8	9	10

CANDLE CREATION LOG

DATE CREATED _____

CANDLE NAME	

INGREDIENTS	AMOUNT	METHOD SUMMARY

OILS & SCENTS	MOLD & FINISH

OVERALL RATING									
1	2	3	4	5	6	7	8	9	10

IMAGE(S) / SKETCHES

NOTES / SUGGESTIONS FOR IMPROVEMENT

BURN LENGTH RATING									
1	2	3	4	5	6	7	8	9	10

CANDLE CREATION LOG

DATE CREATED _____

CANDLE NAME	

INGREDIENTS	AMOUNT	METHOD SUMMARY

OILS & SCENTS	MOLD & FINISH

OVERALL RATING

1	2	3	4	5	6	7	8	9	10

IMAGE(S) / SKETCHES

NOTES / SUGGESTIONS FOR IMPROVEMENT

BURN LENGTH RATING

1	2	3	4	5	6	7	8	9	10

DATE CREATED _____

CANDLE NAME	

INGREDIENTS	AMOUNT	METHOD SUMMARY

OILS & SCENTS	MOLD & FINISH

OVERALL RATING									
1	2	3	4	5	6	7	8	9	10

IMAGE(S) / SKETCHES

NOTES / SUGGESTIONS FOR IMPROVEMENT

BURN LENGTH RATING

1	2	3	4	5	6	7	8	9	10

DATE CREATED _____

CANDLE NAME	

INGREDIENTS	AMOUNT	METHOD SUMMARY

OILS & SCENTS	MOLD & FINISH

OVERALL RATING									
1	2	3	4	5	6	7	8	9	10

IMAGE(S) / SKETCHES

NOTES / SUGGESTIONS FOR IMPROVEMENT

BURN LENGTH RATING

1	2	3	4	5	6	7	8	9	10

CANDLE CREATION LOG

DATE CREATED _____

CANDLE NAME	

INGREDIENTS	AMOUNT	METHOD SUMMARY

OILS & SCENTS	MOLD & FINISH

OVERALL RATING									
1	2	3	4	5	6	7	8	9	10

IMAGE(S) / SKETCHES

NOTES / SUGGESTIONS FOR IMPROVEMENT

BURN LENGTH RATING									
1	2	3	4	5	6	7	8	9	10

DATE CREATED _____

CANDLE NAME	

INGREDIENTS	AMOUNT	METHOD SUMMARY

OILS & SCENTS	MOLD & FINISH

OVERALL RATING									
1	2	3	4	5	6	7	8	9	10

IMAGE(S) / SKETCHES

NOTES / SUGGESTIONS FOR IMPROVEMENT

BURN LENGTH RATING

1	2	3	4	5	6	7	8	9	10

CANDLE CREATION LOG

DATE CREATED _____

CANDLE NAME	

INGREDIENTS	AMOUNT	METHOD SUMMARY

OILS & SCENTS	MOLD & FINISH

OVERALL RATING									
1	2	3	4	5	6	7	8	9	10

IMAGE(S) / SKETCHES

NOTES / SUGGESTIONS FOR IMPROVEMENT

BURN LENGTH RATING

1	2	3	4	5	6	7	8	9	10

NOTES

Made in United States
North Haven, CT
13 January 2025

64398809R00068